For the Within

Maria N. Angelova

MW01002494

Song of Cicadas

monodrama

Maria N. Angelova
& Simeon Dimitrov

NYC
Mar 2023

Contents

The act takes place in a room, covered with a Persian carpet. In the middle of the room on the carpet, there is a tall standing lamp and a pile of furniture consisting of: a rocking chair on which a small classy table is turned upside down, on top of the table sits a basket with yarn balls (each in a different color), next to the basket sits a picture album, leaning next to the rocking chair stands a suitcase, and a small red heart-shaped pillow sits on the chair under the pile of furniture. A CD player is on the floor next to the chair. In the yarn basket, there is also a small pencil and a small pillbox. On the other side of the rocking chair, there is another small classy table on which sits a silver teapot and an elegant teacup with a saucer. On the far back left corner of the carpet, there is an open 3-step ladder and an elegant wine bottle under it. There is a long red scarf hanging on the ladder, a blue scarf hangs on the back of the rocking chair, and another colorful scarf lies on the armrest of the rocking chair. There is a large red pillow on a small step stool in the front right corner of the carpet with a small laptop on it, and another two pillows in the front left corner of the carpet. Behind the carpet, in the middle of the stage, there is a backdrop with a picture of a window on which there are huge cicadas.

K R I S T I N A is an elegant lady dressed in a red sleeveless house robe over a short skirt and a blouse. She is in her fifties. She is a cheerfully optimistic person.

1. You're lighting a fire under me

(Phone rings. Kristina picks up the phone.)

"Hi! ... I was just about to call you ...

(she listens to the person on the phone)

...yes, yes, I'm ready to work with you today...

(she listens to the person on the phone, and responds)

"**How does one** take stock of one's own life?

"Oh, Gosh! You're lighting a fire under me...

"Okay, I got it! Today will be a real work meeting ... Yes! Just as you told me, I have prepared: a chair, a lamp, a basket with yarn balls, a photo album, a table with a laptop... and...

(while placing the table, chair, and small laptop in order, she puts the basket with yarn balls on the side table and the album on the big pillow, and turns on the lamplight)

"I'm starting to write... What should I write

about? MY ..LIFE... How do I even put LIFE into words? Even the one that I have lived in? ... Not that I don't remember it ... unbearably ... day by day ... hour by hour ...

"But... Well, how do I put it into words? As events?... Or as emotions!... Or as lessons? ... Can they even be separated?... Absurd! ...

"Oh, yes, as you told me - I prepared the suitcase... The suitcase I'll be running away with? Why am I running away? Who will I be running from ... Where will I be running to? ... Not that I haven't thought to grab my luggage and ... Oh, so many times! ...

"Maybe I'll be running away from myself?... Wow, you have X-ray vision... You see the whole picture...

"Yes, yes ... I will sit down to write. I won't *(i.e waste time)*. ... And I'm waiting for you to come, okay?"
(she hangs up the phone)

Gosh, how I obey his every instruction! I just feel that I trust him... Anyway, come on now, focus...
(she sits down in front of the laptop and concentrates)

But where do I start from? Life is a tangle ... everything is connected like in a knot. I have to pull the threads out one by one ... Is this why he asked for these yarn balls? And ...to be multi-colored? Oh! Each color will describe the nature of my experience...

Gosh, in what language should I write? Jeez, it's been so long.

What from my life do I tell? And how do I present it? (*takes a moment*)... My blood type is "B positive". In English, it sounds just the same as the phrase "be positive." More so, I'm a "pathological optimist!" People even wonder and... some get angry that I always see something good in any situation and refuse to see the bad things.

I will start with... with my childhood... no, it's boring... With the birth of my children... it's also... With my divorce?!... Oh, God! To live through that again?! No! No! ... I will write about the good moments in my life! And were there any? ... Of course, there were ...

(*she starts typing*)

2. He loved me

He loved me… I loved him too.

"What's your name?" He asks me…

"Kristina. But here at school, they call me Krista."

"Krista!" - he sounded really teasingly. And he reached out his hand. What does he want?

"Congratulations! You have to do theater. Do you want to be part of a theatre group? An actor from the state theater is leading it."

And with this group… We went to a winter camp. Then, to the city and national festivals. Together all the time, on trains and stages. We became friends. People came up with the saying "Five Men and Kristina". I was in love with him, a boy with a great kind heart and he loved me so much.

"Krista, for the high school anniversary we will make a play - 'In the Soft Autumn' by Valery Petrov. I've also written songs for it …"

And I was learning Valery Petrov's poetry:

"Oh, my First Kiss,

I can't forget you to this day, and

I won't mix you with the memory of those

which I have blasted in an endless void.

That memory begins to play again,

each time I think of Love."

(she rests her head on the back of the chair as if going into a beautiful dream)

Yes, that very same year, with my first love... we are walking on the sand by the seashore, the shimmering moon path is right in front of us, the waves are quietly clapping.... His eyes are full of love and admiration, with kindness and devotion .... My little hand gets lost in his palm ... my body is trembling as I feel his body close to mine .... his cozy big palms warm my cheeks, and ... that first thirsty warm sensual kiss fills my whole universe, and ... my heart seems to expand as if about to burst open my chest. After, I wrote about these same warm palms and loving eyes:

"The entire sea is in your palms.

Your eyes are the rise of a bright full moon."

God, what a riddle nature is! What about the nature of man?... God, what kind of being is the woman? What forces are lurking within her? ... Innocent and defenseless, yet persistent and stubborn ... Energies that blind us... brain-fog us! Oh, the Animal Kingdom! Are we indeed animals... Do the chemical processes in us make us light-headed? ... And what about the beast called man? With his brain fog and stubbornness... With energies and forces that are more destructive than floods and fires...

(she continues typing)

Yes, high school ... Those were some of the best years of my life ... And my favorite teacher, my literature teacher. God, this woman loved me so much! "Krista," she tells me, "I see Him looking at you with such love, admiration, and devotion which is very rare in life." ... "I appreciate you so much, Krista! Go, study, make theater. You're smart and ambitious. I know you will be successful. But, remember this from me, nothing can replace a good partner in life. Remember it."...

(she stands, pours some tea into the cup, takes the cup with the saucer, takes a sip, and walks to the front of the carpet)

I didn't remember it... I learned it through my own life experience... and I am sharing it. The good life partner!

Hahaha ... Today in the bookstore I read a book title, "Is there life ... after marriage?"

Is the majority of humanity so unhappy with their partners?! Do others experience what I experienced too? Is the idea of a "good partner" an illusion? ...

(she walks back to the chair, leaving the cup on the side table)

3. Why is so much blood leaking?

How my thoughts jump from one thing to another...

"Go see a doctor, in the ER, in a large hospital, to grab their attention right away! This is no joke!"

What is it? Why is so much blood leaking? What kind of signs is my body giving me this time?

Why didn't I learn to listen to my heart? It has been talking to me all my life ... But I, no, stubborn as a mule; thinking my head knows more! ... God sends you signs. Your body is tearing apart to tell you something, and you .... At least over the years, I've learned to listen to some of the signs...

(she sits on the chair and starts typing on the laptop)

I remember feeling so confused. And, I open the Bible and I read, that if one sins, you can forgive them once or twice, but if you forgive them a third time, you become an accomplice in their sin.

And as I read that, I understand why my son was crying and accusing me: "Mom, you are the same as him. Doesn't matter that you are trying to protect me, you are staying with him, forgiving him, forgiving him for what he is doing to me too. Why are you still living with him? For your convenience, right? You don't care about me... "

And that didn't even shake me to my core enough. Although, it has occurred to me thousands of times, that if a marriage hurts the children, it is damaging.

And really, why did I stay?!

I've been putting it off for so many years ... I wake up the Godfather of my children in the middle of the night, crying... And on the next day, this elderly man meets up with me and asks: "Really, why are you staying with him, Kristina? You don't deserve this. If I was in his place, and you gave birth to three sons, I will be giving you the royal treatment each and every day. Shame on him... But.. you, why did you tolerate such awful treatment for so long?" "Godfather, do you know how much I prayed for him? I always believed that everything would change. And I wanted to have children, too. And they are still young. And I don't know if I can handle everything by myself." "You will be fine. That sort of thing for someone to hit and abuse you ... is intolerable. Go talk to a lawyer and get your affairs straightened out."

Really, why didn't I value myself enough? Why did I stay? Maybe because I was scared ... Or because, when I decided to complain the first time back in Bulgaria, the policeman told me: "Who knows what you did to deserve a hit?".... Or maybe I believed that I could fix him. Why do I think that I have to victimize myself to correct someone ... Yes, the exact word is "victimize"...

Well, the Universe had to hit me on the head and wake me up somehow for me to decide, to take the big step, to say: that's it, no more!....

(visibly disturbed, she gets up, pours some tea in the cup, and swallows a pill...)

4. I went to the point that I got paralyzed

I went to the point that I got paralyzed... I am talking ... while crying... filled with despair and helplessness and ... I feel my shoulders drooping and I become silent....

"Mom ... Tell me what is it with you?"

I feel my body stiffen up. He tries to straighten my shoulders to no avail ... My legs are already numb, but I'm standing up straight as if I'm being rooted to the ground and becoming more and more heavier. He tells me how much he loves me and how sorry he is for what he'd done to me. He sits on the ground in front of me and occasionally wipes my tears.

What happened to me? As if my power switch shut down. That was probably the last straw... He begins to carry me, but my legs drag on the floor. He lays me down on the couch and I can't even move, I feel pain in my back and in my neck. My body shut down... just like computers do - when we overwork them a lot, they freeze up...

"Mom, I'll put on this mantra ... This one is a Buddha mantra"......

These Indian women sing so beautifully......

No, I don't want any water. I do not want anything...

What will I do if this continues? All that I want to do with my life requires my body and my voice - to infuse these people with energy... Such strong and bright energy I once had.... Will I ever be in command of my body again? ... My tears flow down ...

What are these Indian women singing?...

(*surprised*) My leg is moving, here goes one arm and the other one... Here I go, I sit up... slowly...I may even stand up ...

"Oh, Mom!..."

I don't want to talk ... No, I don't want to pick up the phone ... I don't want to look at the screen ... I don't want to! ...

(*She comes back to reality. She looks at the computer and decides to write down her memory.*)

I can write this down.

(*She writes for a while. Then visibly satisfied, she stops, puts on music, starts dancing, and looks at herself in the mirror; an imaginary mirror on the site of the audience.*)

5. How beautiful I am!

Wow, look how beautiful I am. Such a beauty! Well, look how slender I am.

I can straighten my shoulders and suck in my stomach... And with my boobs leading the way. At least, now I have boobs. Look how the self-esteem of a woman is boosted when her boobs start growing...No, no I am not going to slim down.

When will someone draw me? I wanted someone to draw me while my body was ideal. For me, it is still ideal though...

I will tell Larry to photograph me. And not only portraits. With his portraits, I've received 100 marriage proposals. I wonder what would happen if I offered him to photograph me naked?!?

Hmm, if I get undressed in front of him, he will very quickly fall dead. No, that is too risky. I will let the guy live a bit longer. I don't want to rack up any more guilt.

My mother once warned me that I gave my neighbor a heart attack when I showed up at the front door in my mini-short skirt. The poor old man the next day was in the ER with an infarction.

(she is startled)
Oh my, I need to focus on my writing.

(she sits to write)

6. The sun is blazing today

(sounds of cicadas)

Oh, the sun is blazing beautifully today. It's burning my back. The cicadas are as if in a singing competition. Years ago when I first heard that metallic strumming sound of the cicadas, I thought it was some electrical wires short-circuiting. Recently, I learned that they live between one and 17 years underground, and when they crawl out of the ground, they shed their thick-shelled skin and emerge with a new body and a set of wings.

Now, I am sitting in my backyard with my late breakfast and I wholeheartedly admire them. They only make this sound when it's really hot and I feel so good that it is hot, that the sun is shining, and that I can sit in my backyard... in silence.

"Mama, please tell me something, anything... We are going to be alright. I will give you some money. Didn't you tell me that we all need to contribute...We are going to be alright..."

He got scared ...when he saw me in that miserable state. Was I miserable-looking or scary? But he saw me, that even I, the matriarch, can too fall apart and not always be the strong one made of iron and steel.

There he takes out one or two of each from the Omegas, the vitamins, the minerals, the enzymes. They roll down the table; he grabs them quickly from falling off and puts them in the bowl with a peach.

The cicadas are strumming away.

Thank God that he didn't get so frightened to call an ambulance....my son...my child...he truly loves me...
(sounds of cicadas disappear)

For two days in a row, he has been talking a lot about his father. Recently, they have been seeing each other quite a bit... Disappointed, angry, and embittered to such an extent, that he is waking up with nightmares.

"Will he ever stop? How does he not understand that we live with you, you are everything for us, all these years with just you? I have told him many times, "stop talking against our mother." He is downright "delusional." He speaks to me as if I have never lived with you and as if I don't remember what was in the past at home."

"Poor guy! You know, my boy, you can only feel sorry for such a person. A lawyer told him that the family court was not a criminal court and that he could lie without any punishment. I appreciated him for being hardworking, capable, and proactive, and we created such a successful business together... Nevertheless, when one repeats a lie long enough, one starts believing it...

"When psychologists advised him to honestly apologize to me, to show real regret and remorse, and to ask forgiveness for what he had done to me and us, it was so funny.... "I want you to forgive me for what I have caused you .... but..." and began accusing me of how I provoked him... They began to roll their eyes in disbelief...

"He wants to destroy me!?

"My son, do you know what I believe in? What we wish unto others happens to us. You were 3 and 8. It's been so many years. What haven't we gone through? However, as you can see we manage somehow...

"Can't you change the subject when you're talking? Talk about something that he feels flattered about. Tell him: "you have qualities that I value very much, could you tell me more about your projects?" ... Why is it that you only talk about me?"

"I don't want to see him anymore"- my child cries out ...

(The phone rings. She answers the phone.)

"Yes, I am writing, I am writing.....yes, yes...yes, I am waiting for you. See you soon. Thank you!"

7. The gynecologist

(She makes a gesture of remembering something interesting as if saying: "here's what else I'm going to say")

The gynecologist!
(she imitates his funny pompous tone)
"Let's see what's up, my girl. Where do you say it hurts?"
"Down, below the belly."
"Have you been suffering from any infections?"
"From bronchopneumonia …"
"How come, my poor girl, how did you get this pneumonia?"
"It was a February day. A man's house near our high school was burned down in flames right in front of our eyes. His clothes were burned as well. I took off my pullover and gave it to the doctors to dress him up with. Soon after, a cold rain poured with a strong wind, and I got wet, and by the time I got home, I was pretty cold. The sea wind is piercing."

"Let me examine you now …*(she turns towards the rocking chair imitating him as if it is a gynecological examination chair)* Ohhhh, colleagues, come here."

What did this doctor see that he hadn't seen before? And these were his students! Seemingly, he was their professor...

"Look - this is a typical example of an "underdeveloped uterus." The girl is 23 (years old) and her uterus is like an 11-year-old kid's uterus! With such a uterus, she cannot get pregnant. And if she gets pregnant, she won't be able to keep the pregnancy. And her tubes are blocked on one side, so..." *(imitating his arrogance she makes a sign of hopelessness)*

And these students of his bend over to look at me as if I'm an exhibit in a museum ...

And what? What did he just say ... I felt nauseous? It never occurred to me that I would not be able to have children....It is as if the whole world has turned upside down....Just a minute! I already had been pregnant in the past. No, I am not telling this doctor about those two abortions. No! I have no guilt about it. We weren't ready to have kids. He was a sweet boy, but we weren't ready to have a family; I still wanted to go study and get a degree in acting, and he was still a mama's-boy, he wasn't ready to come with me anywhere, and that relationship was doomed altogether. Nevertheless, this doctor is saying that even if I didn't make the abortions I wouldn't have been able to keep the pregnancies anyway!? Oh, no!!!

What is the significance of this university acting program, acting in general, my career???...Gosh, everything is meaningless now... *(she takes a small pencil from the yarn basket and holds it in her hand as if it is a cigarette, and "smokes" through the next monologue)*

Now what? No, no, I will not accept that I cannot have children. I'll have to try. Well, at least I have someone to try with... Not that he is the most suitable person .... We broke up, then we got together again... at least now we are together.... And I loved him ... at some point. Can I truly forgive him for what he caused me....I felt suffocated... I began choking, and then I blacked out, oh my Lord, I thought I was dying... I'm still claustrophobic to this day...How could he have done this to me??? At least he came to tell me that he wanted to take care of me when I was going insane. I actually would've gone crazy... I will tell him that I want to have children... When he came to Sofia to live with me, on the first day he told me that he wanted to have children. Now ... he has changed his mind...Who else can I find? Who else would want me as crazy as I am? Kosio? He tells me that he wants to marry me. Well, how is he going to marry me straight away... I see him, the man looks at me with love in his eyes... but I don't feel anything.... And what is it that binds me to ...*(having in mind the guy who choked her)*

Lord, how confused I am....

(she puts the "cigarette"-pencil back into the basket)

No, I will not accept that I cannot have children.... Even though I never thought about having children, especially while being a student ... However, it seems very appropriate to me now. Yes! Since I am not learning anything from my professor, at least I will focus on trying to conceive a child. That is exactly what I will do…. If I can…. I'll try…. If I believe, it will happen….

(she comes back to the current reality)
And I gave birth to not only one…but…three… boys… My children…

8. November 10:30 am. Was this karma?!

(she sits on the chair and starts typing)

November 10:30 am ... Back in the office of my lawyer on the 20th floor ... Justice raised so high! ... Loads of boxes of our documents everywhere... It's as if I have started a job on this floor ....

Oh, my God! We could have finished five years ago. So much stress, so much time, so much money we wasted. Each of us could have taken our own matters into our own hands and lived life on our own terms. What was the point of all this?.... And how much longer will it go on for?

He has a young girlfriend who lives with him and they're happy. And he bought a building. And I helped him. I made the documents and he got the money from the state for his businesses. What the hell was going through his head? Not to mention how many opportunities we lost and... the kids were driven mad...

The elderly Madame Justice was so angry with him: "What kind of parent are you? Parents think of their children first, but you?"

My lawyer's phone rang. "Kristina, Madam Greer, the judge, wants to see you. Such a thing has never happened - a judge trying to reach my client."

The ceiling is low. It's as if there's a shortage of oxygen. The corridor is small and narrow.

The judge slowly raises her head, and looks at me: "Kristina, I just received a fax from the defendant's lawyer…. at 10:35 am the defendant declared bankruptcy. All of his properties are blocked. Kristina, you are going to have a very difficult year. And maybe not one. There's nothing I can do for you anymore."

(still in a process of understanding and asking herself questions)

Is all this karma? A karmic debt of my family lineage? Once I overheard the story of my father … They were nine children. When their mother was pregnant with the last one, their father - heavily intoxicated and angry at his life - beat her before their eyes … his own sons! But the reaction was fierce. They tie him to a tree and beat him to a pulp, then he falls ill and dies soon afterward. Before he closes his eyes, he curses them!!!! Patricide?! Karma!!! And karma is never too late to appear to ask for payment….

What else is there in store for me???!!!! My kids got to listen to these ugly messages from his creditors early in the morning and seeing me worried on the phone, leaning over papers, and wondering how to deal with all the loans I was left with.

Thank God, at least we're in the house, and I'm sort of handling it all ... Thank God!

(writing on the computer) Thank God!

(puzzled) I guess I took a deep dive into my memories.

Will this story fit in my play???

(her expression is as if saying: "isn't that what I am doing?") Taking stock of my life...

(stands up from the chair, takes an elegant wine bottle from under the ladder, sips from it, and continues holding the bottle...)

9. At last NATFA

And what now? ... *(has an exciting memory, stands up next to the ladder)*

AAAAAt last NATFA, my sought-after National Academy for Theater and Film Arts!!! Such a dream theater academy...So what if I'll be in a dormitory with cockroaches? And if we're three in one room, so what? And there's this Nigerian woman Betty, big personality, raising her chickens in the bathroom!!! And this terrified Vietnamese girl was barely staying in the room at all. But to compensate, Betty added her boyfriend into the mix. We are living our best life, what more can you ask for...

Why didn't I go to talk to Ostrovsky??? And, Ostrovsky, if at every audition round had such a fond look on his face when I was on stage, jumping, grinning, and shouting, "Please declare your love for me", then why didn't he take me in his class??? Sasho Stoyanov didn't even notice me in the crowd. I wasn't to his taste at all, I didn't have big boobs, and I wasn't flirtatious. It was a complete misunderstanding of me being in his class!!! I had to go and ask them to move me. But Boyko told me "don't" and I trusted him.

Ohhhh *(she sits on the upper step of the ladder and goes deep into her thoughts)*

Maybe this also was some kind of trial of fate? ...Weren't they right to tell me that I would not learn anything new at NATFA after playing with such seasoned professional actors?

Kristina, get yourself together! At last, you are at the top university theatre academy. And you will have your degree!......And how incredible is the teacher in opera singing?!...And where else will you be offered classes in opera singing, and at such a high level? Also, there were dance classes, stage combat, and theory classes. What didn't we learn? Education is education! I won't feel like a half-finished product on the theater stages, and I will be able to play anywhere.

Oooo, what a cutie Kiril Popov was in speech class!! He had been a pilot in the war. He was...ahhh...a real nobleman! And with what fatherly love he looked at us and he had so much fun with those tongue twisters. He made it worthwhile for me to stay in this class! A rare good person!

No, no, the fact that I was able to enter the top university theatre academy without any connections, just proves that a person can achieve anything if they desire it long enough and ask for it strongly enough.

(She gets up from the ladder and takes a few steps forward as if leaving that memory behind. Still, with the bottle in her hands, she takes a sip.)

10. The Angel

God, is this a visit from heaven's angels?!

(*going towards the ladder, she leaves the bottle on the small table, and starts reciting her poem as if in a trance while slowly stepping up on the ladder*)

Do not ignore me
Do not underrate me.
I am the Angel within you!

I'm bigger than all your little
earthly compares with others.
Have faith in me, and
don't stick me in the closet!
Do not lock me in the dark!

Place me on display!

Lift me and wave me like a flag.
Leave me like a bamboo
fast and furious to grow up,
so high, that even you see me.

And all the way to the Stars We go!

Let the wind burst us,
let the sun burn us ...
In the ecstatic rhythm of the vortex,
with you I will dance,
with you, my precious Princess!
I've chosen You to journey with!
I've chosen You among the Stars!

Trust me! – it's not You carrying me,
but by me, you are carried!
Have faith, have faith in the beat,
have faith in me and yourself.

I am the Angel within you.

Like a cicada, I break up
your hard brown dead shell.
Winter is over! I throw it away!
And finally free, I emerge!

The wings and the voice,

you do have them;
I saved them within you.
Here we go, we fly up together!
And in a duet with the crickets,
we warm up the soul of the summer!

We are the vortex,
we dance in the rhythm.
Trust your voice and trust your wings!

And have faith in the song you do carry.

I have only you to be in this dance.
I am the Angel,
that
You are!

(by this time she is on the top of the ladder, and at the end of the recitation, as if coming back to reality, she sits on the steps of the ladder)

11. We learn throughout our whole lives

(She gets up and starts piling up the furniture on the chair as if giving up. She moves the ladder to the other side, takes the yarn basket, and puts it on the floor in front of the stool. She sits on the stool and starts playing with the purple yarn.)

"Mom, you've been deluding yourself that you're alright. You are riddled with issues and problems..."

(The phone rings. She does not answer it for a while. She stands up, takes the end of the yarn thread, leaving the ball to unravel, and goes towards the table where the phone is. She puts the thread across the table and picks up the phone.)

"Yes... Hello, my boy! I was just thinking about what you said... That I'm not alright... Listen to me, my child... Many truths are prehistoric. And one of them is that the highest power is Love.

"I'm sorry what? You're inviting me for tea? Okay, I accept, but a little later... Forgive me..."

I have been telling my boys for a long time: we

learn throughout our whole lives! And the more we learn, the more we want to know. And for me, it's like quenching a thirst.

Each time I hear new things, I learn new pearls of wisdom and truths about life, about myself, and how LIFE works. We only hear what we are ready to hear though.... It's like the words in a foreign language. If we don't know the word, we don't even hear it. The same goes with ideas ...

It is an ancient wisdom that we become what we think. The discipline of our thoughts is the most important discipline we have to master.

Yes, we become what we think.

FEAR is the devil who can rob us of everything if we do not defeat it.

If you continue to think of yourself as unhappy and poor, you will end up being unhappy and poor.

I see myself as being rich and happy. And I am just that. I have three sons. And I am proud of them. And I'm proud of myself...

But how do I get ... into my Flow? There is no point in trying to swim against the current. If something is very painful for you to do, it is in vain for you to continue to torment yourself, rather you must think about whether you are not going against your own current. I have done so much to prove the opposite.

We must do what we love, where our hearts lead us to, and what people seek and admire us for. Everyone has a unique place in this world, there isn't any competition.

"The grass doesn't try to grow - it just grows.
The fish doesn't try to swim - it just swims.
The flower doesn't struggle to bloom - it just blooms.
The bird doesn't try to fly - it just flies."
(Indian proverb)

The angels are giving me a sign that they are next to me.... with this feather...

(she finds a little feather on the table and picks it up)

12. Rhodope

This is like a mantra for me, yes, it is a deep belief within me:

(as she says the following line, she walks towards the window with the cicadas, extending her arms to the side while holding the sides of her robe like wings)

"I am infinitely happy and successful! Whatever I have wanted, I have achieved and I am continuing to do so! My every dream…"

(she begins to spin around in blissful ecstasy taking her robe off in one turn and putting it on the back of the chair)

Casting Announcement. Looking for a young actress. And …

"Kristina, out of the 50 women in the competition, we chose you. Congratulations! The role is very demanding. Valentina. Meanwhile, you will also need to quickly get into the role of Raina in the play "The Female Kingdom". And the tours begin soon."

Joy … and … Splendour…

I fell in love with this mountain. The rocks are picturesque with images and figures. Autumn is magical, with so many colors. And autumn is my favorite season, I just feel like I am falling in love. In the theater, most of them are older. I am like a little girl amongst them. They even laugh at me saying: "You can't even drink a shot of vodka ?!" "Well, I can't!"

And one evening, one of them comes to my apartment saying he wants to be with me. "What?!? Get lost! Go home!"

"You can't still be a virgin, right?!!!"

"Even if I am not... you have no place here!"

"Aw, come on girl, then why are you giggly with everyone and acting all flirtatious. You give off a lot of wrong signs."

We are rehearsing with Velik Slavov. He's so old! 34 years old... a gorgeous actor and a brilliant stage partner, such a joy!!! Premiere! Applause. Standing ovations. The critics are delighted. ... And on the streets of the city.... I need bodyguards....

(she takes the big pillow, hugs it, and turns around like in a dance)
I feel that I am not on the ground, but a foot above it. The magic of the theater... And I - in it...

13. Giving birth

(puts the pillow on the floor and sits on it)
I spoke with Rosi. She is an astrologer. I asked her what the stars say, which day is better. She told me that both are good, only that I should give birth at noon.

"Will you be able to drive me on Wednesday?" I ask my husband. "And …. will you be able to take care of the child? He's big, almost 9 already, he can take care of himself. He even cooks!" Gosh, how much this kid had to learn while I was lying down and couldn't even move!
"I'll drive you. And I'll stay during the delivery. I want to videotape, too."
"Are you sure you want to watch???"

Wow, what a tiny little room. A claustrophobic person can drop dead here.
"I will sit here and read my newspapers." (*pointing to the imaginary husband*)

Oh…. it's starting to hurt. Yeah, here come the contractions. And he is flipping through his newspapers. He has nothing to worry about! He is neither getting pregnant, neither holding the pregnancy nor is he giving birth. What do men even know …

"Please - call the midwife, push that button" ...

Is he going to reach through me??? "What did you even push? My bed is lifting my legs, oh gosh, it hurts a lot, and this bed is folding me in half... What did you do? Now my head is rising. (*in a panic*) You completely folded me... Please straighten this bed! Oooohh ... Someone has to come ... I am in labor..."

"What's going on?" - the midwife looks at me very angrily. "You can't give birth, your water broke half an hour ago."

"Well, I've been here on this IV since this morning."

"You're early. We'll bring the anesthetic to put in your back."

"I don't want any anesthetic."

"Why, are you Jewish?"

"I'm not Jewish - I just don't want anything in my back. Please, it hurts, take a look."

(*she turns her back to the audience, and her legs are in a bent position as if in labor*)

"Let me see.... AAAAAA, the baby is coming out."

Ahhh, now she's in a hurry.

"Hurry, Daddy! Help bring the bed to the maternity ward."

Bamm, they slammed my bed into the door so hard?! That's all I needed right now!!!

"Breathe! Breathe! The doctor has to come from downstairs."

"Doctor, I need to poo."

"Don't worry, poo away. Just keep pushing. I need to make a little incision in one place so that the baby can come out easier. A bit more, push ... ehhhh... *(she turns towards the audience, still sitting on the floor, holding an imaginary baby in her hands)* What a beautiful boy. I can see he will be a rich man, he is covered with all this fat, see that white on top? They say when a baby is born covered with fat it will become a rich man. May your baby live long and be healthy!"

"May my children live long and be healthy..."

14. Monaco

(sitting on the floor, takes the yellow yarn ball and starts playing with it, unraveling it)

They deprived me of having any job in the arts and culture sector... for political reasons.... And ... the paradox was...that the next day they called me in... Oh, they needed me for something ...

We are going in with my husband... Why is he coming with me anyway? ...To follow me?....

The director politely looks at me and says:

"Kristina, we are invited to perform in Monaco - in an international theater festival. It is organized by the royal family...We have a problem though....The actress is pregnant. Will you be able to take on the role of Edith Piaf? There's a lot of text, singing, and dancing..."

My husband immediately pipes in: "I will not allow her to travel without me."

I am trembling...

The director nods, "We'll take him, too."

"Okay, let's try this."

....

We are rehearsing. ... At home, the phone rings.

(she takes the yellow yarn ball next to her ear like a phone)

"Kristina? So you will be going to Monaco, right?"

"Who is calling?"

"We are calling from the 6th Division of State Security. Just know if you don't come back, your child will disappear. Make up your mind wisely."... *(she drops the yarn ball from her hand behind her back)*

Shivering chills are running through my body ...

(she opens the photo album and looks at the pictures as she speaks the following)

We are traveling by bus. We're stopping in Venice. Gondolas!!!.... For the first time, I am stepping into Western Europe.

Here's Monaco down there. What a miraculous view! Am I dreaming??!!! ... Where is my professor now who was telling me: "some are born for lead roles, and you are not." Where is he now to see me where I will be playing? A lead role!

Two friendly women introduce themselves to us in Russian.

"Welcome! You will be performing at the Salle Garnier, two nights, tickets are all sold out." OH, GOD, playing in the Auditorium of the Salle Garnier, the famous Opera House!!!!! The Auditorium is full!! The audience is in awe. I am playing the show in Bulgarian, and these people are crying and laughing with me. God, I am playing in front of the French, and I am portraying their national treasure, Edith Piaf ...

Oh, my big dance finale ... What were the steps again ... do I remember them? ... Doesn't matter, I will improvise ... it's modern ballet, who knows what's after what ... And the last scene, I am dying ...and the audience is sobbing ... crying ... They get on their feet and the applause just doesn't stop. And I bow!!! (*bowing*)

Oh, what an unending joy this festival is. Someone taps me on my shoulder. I turn around. This guy must be two meters tall and I look like a doll next to him. He starts speaking to me slowly in English. "I wanted to make sure you are real. You were an incredible Edith!!!"

Tons of fun. So many people. At the workshop, there are directors, thespians, amateurs, professionals from all over the world. We exchange phone numbers, addresses, hugs.

Second performance. The audience is on their feet. Just an incredible sensation! The auditorium is divine!

(*she closes the album and throws it to the side*)
"Pack everything in! We are hitting the road after the party, at 4 in the morning."

They touch me on the shoulder, the two sisters, the translators.

"Kristina, we live in Amsterdam. We are inviting you to come with us to Holland. We'll introduce you to the theaters and you will play there. You have a place to live, our house is big. We will even find a job for your husband ..."

"We are leaving…"

"Let them leave. You stay. "

"Our child is in Bulgaria."

"We'll take him with the Red Cross."

I see in my periphery two pairs of eyes watching me very closely, two of our people.

"No, I can't stay. I have to go back."

"We will write down our phone number and address in Holland for you."

"Thank you … But … I think I'm being watched and if I take it, I'll be in big trouble."

"We wish you success! Let us hug you. You were incredible!"

(she takes the magenta yarn ball and starts unraveling it)

And only three months later, a letter arrives from the United States.

"The Theater Faculty of the University of Michigan invites you to participate in the International Theater Workshop with another 34 representatives from 17 countries. Please confirm your participation."

(she drops the yarn ball on the floor and puts the thread across the chair)

When something is assigned to you from the Universe, from God --- it finds its way to you …

15. Mamoo

(She rearranges the chair, the lamp, and the table. She takes a small red pillow from the chair and puts it on the table next to the laptop. She sits in deep thought to start writing.)

Oh, God.... Oh, God ...

(she starts writing)

...We were supposed to arrive before 12:30 at night.

God, how will I look at this child? With how much reproach will he look at me? Will he recognize me at all? What is he going to say? Would he want to speak with me at all?

"Mom, why did you leave me? You left me and you went somewhere." Is this what he really thinks or is he citing his grandmother? What did they fill his head up with, my darling boy? My sweet little boy!!!

It's been 13 months and 20 days since we left. I thought I wouldn't last 3 months without him, my dear child. In the fourth month, I lost consciousness and I was taken by ambulance to the hospital. He was born during Chernobyl. I was in fear of how he would be born, if he would be whole ... So many children were born then without hands, without vital organs. When he was born, I didn't ask if it was a boy or a girl, but rather if everything was all there. My sweetheart! ...

Didn't I do it all for him; to live in normal conditions?

My mother, how will she be? She isn't one of the most patient people.

We are approaching Niagara.

God, what will I explain to them at the border? I have to enchant them somehow. I will show them that we have legal refugee status, that we are accepted by the Canadian government, and that this is our child. Somehow, I feel comfortable that people here are understanding. But... my child and my mother do not have visas for Canada... This is downright illegal... Joanna, an American nun, without even knowing me, agreed to invite my mother and my child to come to the States. She said she would meet them at the Buffalo Airport and bring them to the border...

The border checkpoint ... "Here's the document", I explain. "Our child is coming tonight." Two officers, at this midnight hour, are looking at me grinning, as if they are not taking me seriously. "All right, all right, sit there and wait!"

I see a vehicle approaching, I'm all sweaty. It turns out to be a private car.... They let them in... And no one else seems to be coming ...

(she remains in her memory, stops typing, and continues her story as if reliving it)

The bridge is dark.

What could have happened? My mother had shown such heroism to embark on such a journey. She had gone to the US Embassy in Bulgaria and, with such coolness and incredible luck, was given US visas using the invitation from Joanna to some festival...

On the bridge in the distance, I see some lights... It's a cab ... It's approaching ...The officer comes out from the checkpoint booth. The car stops next to the officer. The driver is a huge man. He is so huge that I cannot see if there are people behind him. The officer seems to not understand something the driver says. And this huge man is speaking so quietly as if he is trying to justify himself... The officer becomes very annoyed with the documents. Then, it's as if I hear my mother's voice, speaking something in Bulgarian. I get closer.

I see that in the middle of the back seat my mother is squeezing my child in her arms and her mouth and eyes are wide open in shock....

My, my, he is a big boy!!! He was only three and a half when we left .. Gosh, he has grown so much!

Suddenly our eyes meet, and he screams with all his might, "MAAAAAAMOOOOOO"....

My mother is squeezing him, and he struggles to tear himself away.

Thank God, he recognized me!

"Don't worry my baby, mommy is here, don't worry."

"MAAAAAAMOOOO!!!!!!!"

"Keep this child in its place," the officer screams towards the cab. Then, turning to me, "You stay there behind the pillar!" shouting over mine and my child's cries which I can no longer control...

"MAAAAAMMOOOOO," his voice is both a scream and a cry, desperate to get out of that car ...

Even though I want to reassure him, along with him I cry and scream, "Soon, my Angel, soon."

The officer cannot believe this ... He turns to me and shouts angrily, "Take this child," and he opens the door of the car.

I approach, my child jumps out of the cab and throws himself into my arms. (she grabs the small red pillow from the table and hugs it)

My mother remains sitting in the back seat. It is bluish-black around her whole mouth from all the tension.

God, is this woman going to be okay? She waves at me and says, "Goodbye! I'm leaving." She had fulfilled her promise.

The child holds my face and looks at me. He says, "Mamo," as if he cannot believe it's me. "Mamooooo..."...

(she stands, puts the small pillow on the chair, and starts rocking it like a baby)

16. My Mother

(she takes the black yarn ball and walks in a circle around the room, letting the thread down)

I hated them... I hated my father. I even hated my mother at one point. I hated my husband.

The hatred became a burden to me. It was strange to me that even the Bible says, "Love your enemy." Yes, I felt them just like enemies.

My mother and father hadn't talked to each other for years before they finally divorced. They talked through me. "Krista, tell this to your father." "Krista, tell that to your mother"... My father made good money, but he gave little at home and my mother worked at two places, in a store, and on a construction site during the weekend, and from there she would bring my sister and me the food they would give her for her lunch.

(she leaves the black thread and yarn ball on the floor, and takes the pink yarn ball)

I understood how much my mother loved us.

(she goes around the room leaving the pink thread around)

I have always admired her for her spirit. Always

very well dressed, with her hairstyle, makeup, mani-cure, unlike me... Everyone admires her. She sings very well, she is a singer, she loves to have guests, to cook, to bring food to people, to host a party, to dance. Always helping someone. Many people love her. "Do some good, and forget about it, let it go. It will still catch up to you".. is her motto. As children, my sister and I sang with her full-throated while we cleaned and did laundry. And what a good joke-teller she is?! A very colorful person-ality. Wherever she goes, people remember her and al-ways ask me about her.... and send their many regards and greetings her way.

(leaves the pink yarn ball in the basket)

17. My Father

(she takes the blue yarn ball and starts unraveling it as she is walking around)

My father was a celebrity in our town. As early as eighth grade, when I entered the language high school, my classmates thought that because of him, the teachers were treating me with such respect.

He loved me dearly. He had two post-secondary degrees, he read a lot, he would wake up every morning at 4 to read. He told me that he used to tend the oxen along the river Maritza and that till the age of 9 he wasn't able to read. He stopped smoking at 9. We spoke on philosophical topics. He had more than 3000 volumes of books. I loved delving into those books. He took them with him after the divorce... My sister and I stopped talking to him... Then...he did even more stupid things... I hadn't seen him or heard from him for more than 15 years when I went to Bulgaria for a visit. I went to see him, but he was no longer himself. The next day he died. It was a hot August Day - The Day After The Assumption of Mary. *(she drops the yarn ball on the floor)*

(she takes the laptop and sits on the small stool, and starts writing)

Love is the building block of all energy. Only love, gratitude, and forgiveness can save us. I imagine them: my father, my mother, and my ex-husband as children, young, with pure souls who just want to be loved. I hug them and forgive them... and I ask them for forgiveness...

God, what memories I dug up! I hadn't thought about all this for years ...

18. The curse

(she goes back to the chair, sits there, puts the laptop on the table, and starts writing while laughing)

In the Rhodope Mountains, I got to acquaint myself with more strange, more mysterious things ... For the first time, I saw a man who was bewitched. I learned a lot; curses, spells, incantations, and magic are very powerful energetic tools, real weapons. I realized I could do them too. If it's for a good reason, fine. But if it's for a bad one ... it's scary. I swore I wouldn't curse nor do any bad spells... because with the ball of bad energy you never know if it will come back to haunt you.

Haha Haha

But I had a very funny experience. Well, the experience was pretty sad, but then, each time I remember it, I laugh.

I had told my husband about what I had learned in the Rhodope Mountains.

One night, he had come back with a rather nasty conscience. I saw some pictures, ... I was about to go ballistic. He was acting all important and told me that he must go to bed ...

I am breastfeeding our baby. And he... oh, I just had it up to here... my gloves were off!

"I don't know this woman." *(imitating his guilty tone)*

"Swear on your children's life!" *(imitating herself in anger)*

"I swear on my children's life!"

Well, at this point, I couldn't stand it anymore... I had the feeling that he had sprinkled my kids with embers.

"May your genitals dry up!" I just threw my curse at him like a knife. He was furious. He didn't even try to hit me ... He was just rooted to his spot. He threatened me:

"I'll call the police."

Indeed, he did call the police.

(takes the ladder towards the center-right side of the carpet and sits on it)

About twenty minutes later, two police officers arrive.

"Are you Kristina? A complaint has been called against you? Your husband has called us."

"Well then, let him tell you what he called you for."

We're in the living room, the four of us, standing. They turn to him.

"What did your wife do to you? What happened?"

"She was angry with me and she...cursed me."

"And she ... what???"

"And cursed me."

"I don't understand. Did she tell you something or do something to you?"

"She cursed me. She told me something. But it's equal to doing something to me."

"And what did she tell you?"

He, a little embarrassed, but decisively declared: "She told my genitals would dry up!"....

A long silence... One cop could barely keep himself from laughing... The other kept it together with a lot of self-control and acting mastery: "And ... and ... have your genitals dried up, sir?"

"I do not know!"

"Well, how do you not know? Do you have your genitals intact, can't you check yourself?"

I look away so that I don't burst out laughing. They seriously explained to him that he should be examined if necessary. And then, barely keeping themselves from laughing, they explained to him that since there was no damage yet, they could not hold me responsible ...

19. The men in my life

(sips from the bottle, takes off her blouse leaving the camisole on)

The men in my life....
The men I've been with?
There weren't so many .... No, no ...
My lovers... There weren't so many either.
This is all very personal. Do I indeed want to share it?.... Maybe not...

(playing with the scarves and covering herself with them)

"You give the impression of being quite naughty, but..." *(imitating the guy from the 6th Division)*
"But I am a virgin." *(imitating her younger self)*
"I want to be with you before my wedding day"... he says ...
"Well, I don't. I'm not dating a married man." *(imitating her younger self)*

My picture that was on the wall in the theater had disappeared. It was gone. The guy from the 6th Division of State Security told me he took it.
"What will you tell your wife???"

"You can't still be a virgin? You're already a student in Sofia."

"Yes, I am still one. And for how long will you keep calling me to ask me?"

"They appointed me to be in charge of dealing with prostitution in the area, and I wanted to freshen up my ears. I can't believe there are girls like you still around. You are like a blue diamond."

(imitating a man from her more mature life, she lies down on the pillows on the floor, covering and uncovering herself with the scarf)

"You are so hot! They say that gypsies are like that..."

(she sits, puts the corners of the width of the scarf under her camisole straps, making the scarf look like a dress; and while still on the floor she continues with the following thoughts)

I cannot imagine being with someone just like that, without loving him, just for the momentary pleasure, no, no ... it's not me, it's not for me. And I'm sure because I tried doing it when I was younger. It doesn't work for me. I can't cheat either. I tried doing that too. That totally didn't work for me ... Ha ha ha...

Being in love hurts me. A real physical pain. I feel as if something goes somewhere under my heart and nests there. It hurts me and yet it makes me feel good. Such masochism! ... And then I'm magnetized, I want to be with him, to be near him, to do things with him, to talk with him, to plan with him, to dream with him ... I'm ready to go the distance to be together, to deprive myself of sleep just to be together.

(she recites Emily Dickinson's poem while slowly getting up from the floor)

If you were coming in the Fall,
I'd brush the Summer by
With half a smile, and half a spurn,
As Housewives do, a Fly.

If I could see you in a year,
I'd wind the months in balls---
And put them each in separate Drawers,
For fear the numbers fuse---

If only Centuries, delayed,
I'd count them on my Hand,
Subtracting, til my fingers dropped
Into Van Dieman's Land,

If certain, when this life was out---
That yours and mine, should be
I'd toss it yonder, like a Rind,
And take Eternity---

But, now, uncertain of the length
Of this, that is between,
It goads me, like the Goblin Bee---
That will not state--- its sting.
(Emily Dickinson)

I believe that physical intimacy makes us kins,

and that is a responsibility to me and my soul.

(*Kristina exits the stage.*)

20. The Will

(a recording of Kristina's voice of the following Will plays in the background with musical underscoring)

"Children, ... I will include in my will my last wishes:

1. I see myself leaving this life at the age of 138, in 2099...

2. I don't want to be buried in a grave. Donate my body to scientists, universities or hospitals to be used for research and health needs.

3. Dedicate a bench in my name along the lake, sea, or ocean - and have it look out at the water. Engrave on it: "Dedicated to Mom", and also "Sit here, look at the water, and listen to the birds!"

When you want to remember me, go there and sit on the bench.

4. To commemorate my sending off, play the music of Albinoni... Be merry, serene...
Think of me with joy...

"I'll be around and will dance with you!

"That's all! I love you! I am filled with joy to be your mother. I even named the star in my name in the star registry, not with my full name, but simply, 'Kristina, mother of...... my children!' "

21. I am ready to go

(Kristina enters dressed in an elegant long dress and a light coat, with a long white wig, looking graceful. She goes next to the ladder and leans on it.)

I hear Luna:

"Kristina, what's going on with all your plans? You know, you are making a big mistake and you are passing that on to your sons. You start too many things at a time! ... Start one thing, bring it to its highest level, then start another!"

(she takes the ladder and moves it to the front center of the stage, and leans on it again)

She's right. I am inspired to do a lot of things. I have so many ideas. And I am always wondering what not to do? I am blessed with so many talents and skills, and I never stop learning. Though, for a long time now, I was dreaming of having a show too...

To make my own play... but I don't know how!

(Phone rings. She finds it on the small table, picks it up, and listens...)

"What? Am I ready? I wrote some things ...

"Taking stock of my life? Hahaha... Did I do it? ... I tried...

"Excuse me???

"Won't we be working? Didn't you promise?

"You are leaving !??? What do you mean you're leaving?

"What? I should put my most essential things in the suitcase???

"You got a ticket!? For where? Two tickets??? ...

"You're coming to get me? ...

"... Hello... Hello... Hello..."

(*sounds of Cicadas*)

(*for a moment or two she looks around, takes the suitcase, and thinks about what else to take, and takes nothing; and as if remembering something joyful she hears the cicadas, and makes the following statement...*)

... The song of the cicadas!

(*Kristina rolls the suitcase towards the ladder, puts the suitcase aside, and slowly climbs up the ladder one step at a time while reciting Emily Dickinson's poem*)

TIE the strings to my life, my Lord,
Then I am ready to go!
Just a look at the horses—
Rapid! That will do!

Put me in on the firmest side,
So I shall never fall;

For we must ride to the Judgment,
And it's partly down hill.

But never I mind the bridges,
And never I mind the sea;
Held fast in everlasting race
By my own choice and thee.

Good-by to the life I used to live,
And the world I used to know;
And kiss the hills for me, just once
Now I am ready to go!

(Emily Dickinson)

(At the end of the poem Kristina is on the top of the ladder, as if flying towards her beautiful new life. Lights dim to dark. When the lights come back, Kristina is not there.)

The End

Acknowledgement

I'll be forever grateful to my co-author, my mentor, my director, and my teacher, Simeon Dimitrov, for his faith in me, for his encouragement, for his wholehearted devotion in creating this play and the performance. I am grateful for his trust in me even when I didn't trust in myself at all. His devotion to the process, his professionalism, his big heart, and his endless creativity made me have faith in myself and my creative talent. Working with Simeon Dimitrov changed my life completely and forever! I feel Blessed! That means the world to me!

I am grateful to my partner, the artist George Yaneff, for his unconditional love, for his patience and enormous help in any step on the journey of creating this play, rehearsing, performing, touring, and translating it, from giving me a place to rehearse, to working on the set design, designing the poster and the program, designing the book cover, and much much more. He is not only an incredibly talented artist, but he is an amazing human being, with a warm loving heart and a compassionate soul, full of love! He showed me what love is! His love changed my life forever. And I will be forever grateful to him!

I am deeply grateful to my son Vitan, who is born and lives in Canada. I am grateful to him for learning the Bulgarian language with great detail and deep understanding; for nagging me to teach him proper Bulgarian since his childhood, and even driving me crazy by constantly asking me to correct or approve of his Bulgarian. I am grateful that he became an actor and has a full understanding of theater and literature. I am grateful to him for the translation of this play into the English language. This means the world to me!

I am grateful to my mom Penka and my sons Aleko, Vitan, and Yoan for their unconditional love, wholehearted support, loving encouragement, and passionate cheering throughout the whole process from writing to touring this play. That meant the world to me!

I am grateful to all the people who came into my life for a season, for a reason, or for life, and who enriched my life with lessons and experiences that shaped me to be the person that I am now.

I am grateful to the audience of my performances and, you, the readers of this play for your faith in me, for your laughter and your tears, for your joyful cheering, for your warm compassion, and your cheerful applauses! You make this work meaningful. This means the world to me!

Canada Council Conseil des arts
for the Arts du Canada

I am sincerely grateful to the Canada Council for the Arts for believing in me and seeing value in the play "Song of Cicadas", and funding the translation of it from Bulgarian into the English language. This means the world to me!

Yours lovingly,

Maria N. Angelova

About The Author

Simeon Dimitrov

 Simeon Dimitrov, is a prominent Bulgarian director, poet, and theater pedagogue. He has created more than 200 theater shows. He has published 9 poetry books. He has been awarded the highest national awards as a director and a poet. He helped more than 15 actors write their own shows based on real-life stories. He has been teaching acting for several years. Two of his students were nominated for the 2021 Oscars: Maria Bakalova for a supporting role, and Ilian Ivanov as a producer of a short film.

His book, "The Transformation or the Play of Becoming Another: The Actor's Grammar," was published in 2020, exploring his life-long experience and the latest research in the area of the human mind in connection with acting. In 2020, he was awarded as an Honorable Citizen of the city of Burgas, Bulgaria, where he lives with his family.

About The Author

Maria N. Angelova

Maria N. Angelova is a Bulgarian-Canadian actress and author. She became a professional actress at the age of 18 playing numerous lead dramatic and comedy roles in Bulgarian state theaters. She received a diploma as a Bibliographer from the Institute for Library Science, in Sofia, Bulgaria. She received a degree in Acting for Theater and Film from the National Academy for Theater and Film Arts, in Sofia, Bulgaria. Since 1990, she lives in Canada where she became certified and has worked as a Financial Consultant. After more than 25 years out of her dream acting career, she returns to acting. She created the program Acting Classes for Joy and Life Skills, created a YouTube channel with storytelling, and has performed in theaters and films.

In 2018, Maria wrote more than 100 pages of real-life stories, based on which, together with Simeon Dimitrov, they created the play "Song of Cicadas". The play was directed by Simeon Dimitrov in which Maria performed, and the premiere was in Toronto in December 2018. She has performed it in Canada, the USA, and Bulgaria.

In 2021, the play was translated into the English language by her son, Vitan Pravtchev, who is a young Canadian-born actor, fluent in the Bulgarian language.

SONG of CICADAS © 2021
A bravely honest confessional account
of an immigrant woman, mother, actress, and wife,
filled with humor, drama, erotica, and wisdom
Monodrama by
Maria N. Angelova and Simeon Dimitrov

translated from Bulgarian by Vitan Pravtchev
cover design by George Yaneff

The translation is funded by
the Canada Council for the Arts

Canada Council   Conseil des arts
for the Arts   du Canada

Links

Access Maria's work and contact information here:
https://linktr.ee/MariaNAngelova

Feel free to leave a review and rating on Amazon here:
https://www.amazon.ca/dp/B09BGHWBKS/

We appreciate all your feedback!

Manufactured by Amazon.ca
Bolton, ON